OLDIES *but* GOODIES

American Popular Songs for Solo Piano

arranged by

Geoffrey Haydon

and

James Lyke

edited by

Robert Pace

Arrangements of compositions used by permission of copyright owner
STIPES PUBLISHING LLC
Champaign, IL

Whispering

words and music by **John Schonberger,**
Richard Coburn, and **Vincent Rose**
arr. by **Geoffrey Haydon**
and **James Lyke**

Moderately ♩ = 90–100

Whis - per - ing while you cud - dle near me,

Whis - per - ing so no one can hear me

ped. simile

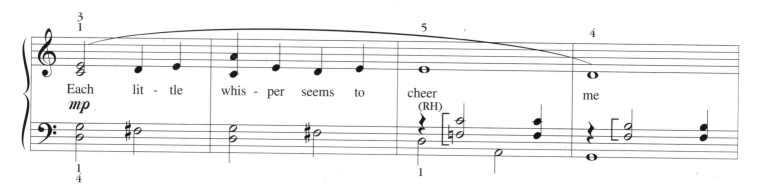

Each lit - tle whis - per seems to cheer me

I know it's true There's no one dear but you, You're

rit.

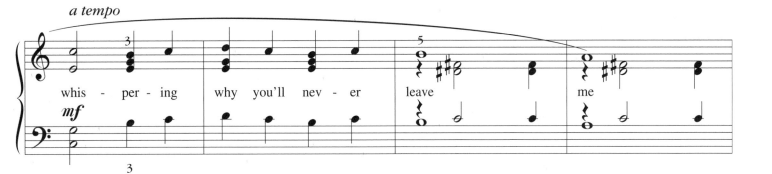

whis - per - ing   why you'll nev - er   leave   me

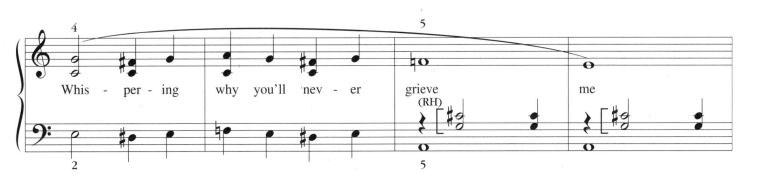

Whis - per - ing   why you'll nev - er   grieve   me

Whis - per and   say that you be - lieve   me

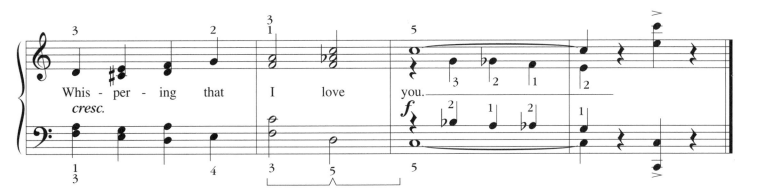

Whis - per - ing   that   I   love   you.

Look For The Silver Lining

words by **Buddy DeSylva**
music by **Jerome Kern**
arr. by **Geoffrey Haydon**
and **James Lyke**

Slowly with expression

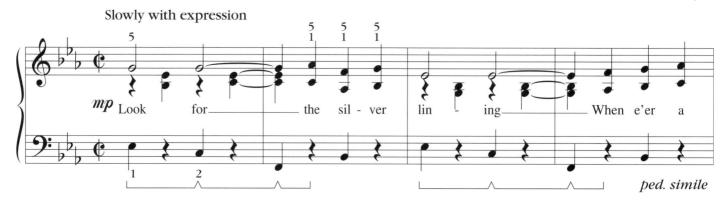

Look for the sil - ver lin - ing When e'er a

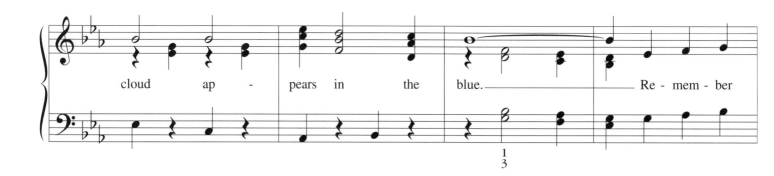

cloud ap - pears in the blue. Re - mem - ber

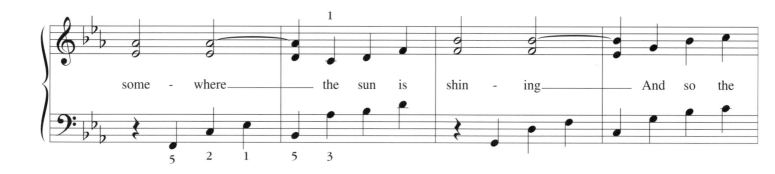

some - where the sun is shin - ing And so the

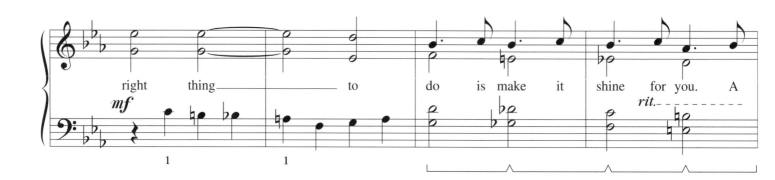

right thing to do is make it shine for you. A

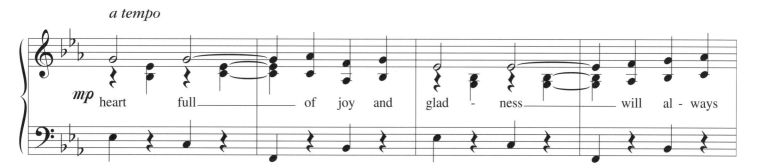

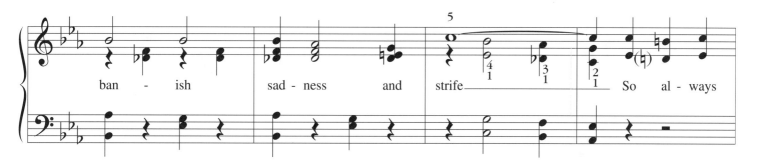

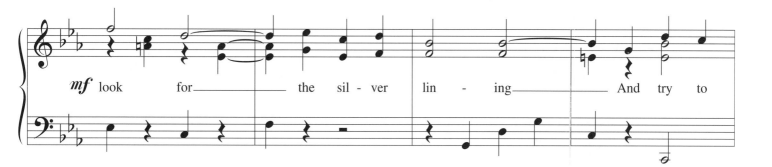

Avalon

words by **Al Joson** and **B. G. DeSylva**
music by **Vincent Rose**
arr. by **Geoffrey Haydon**
and **James Lyke**

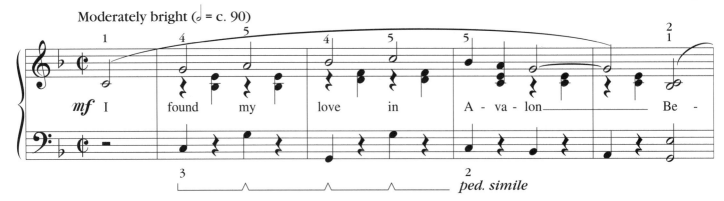

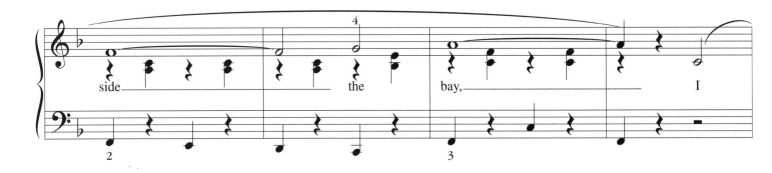

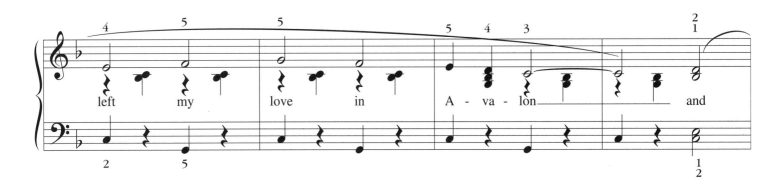

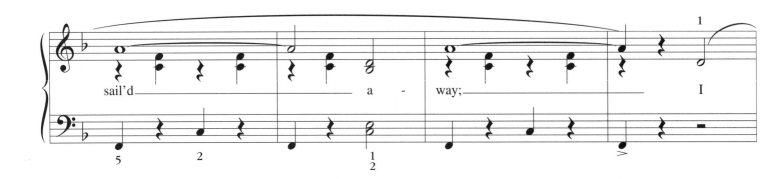

dream   of   her   and   A - va - lon⸺   From

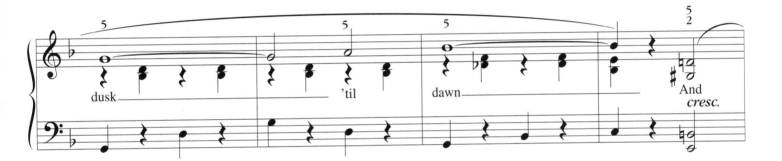

dusk⸺   'til   dawn⸺   And
cresc.

so   I   think   I'll   tra - vel   on⸺   *f* To

A -   va -   lon.⸺

By The Beautiful Sea

words by **Harold R. Atteridge**
music by **Harry Carroll**
arr. by **Geoffrey Haydon**
and **James Lyke**

Moderately fast

By the sea, by the sea, by the beau - ti - ful sea,___ you and

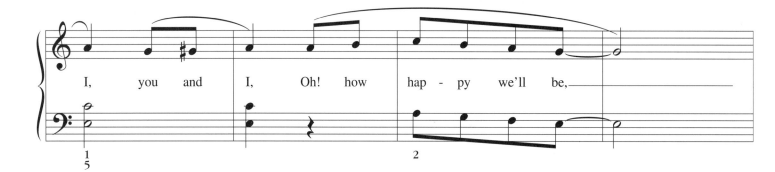

I, you and I, Oh! how hap - py we'll be,___

When each wave comes a - roll - ing in, we will

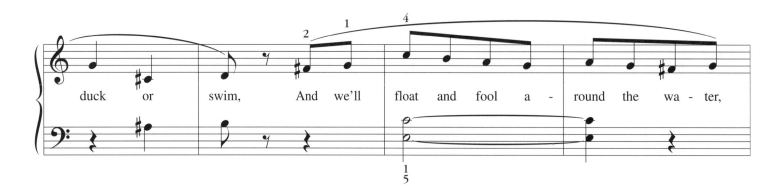

duck or swim, And we'll float and fool a - round the wa - ter,

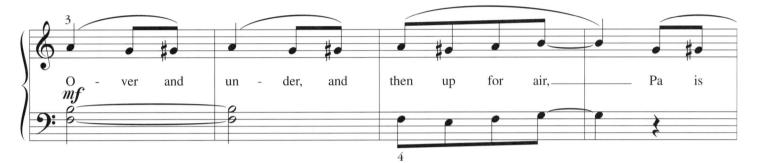

O - ver and un - der, and then up for air,_____ Pa is

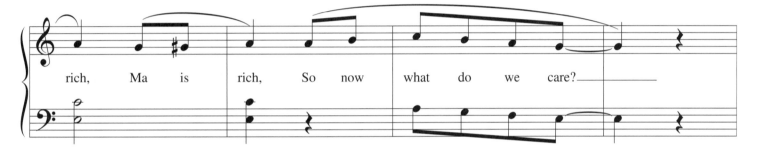

rich, Ma is rich, So now what do we care?_____

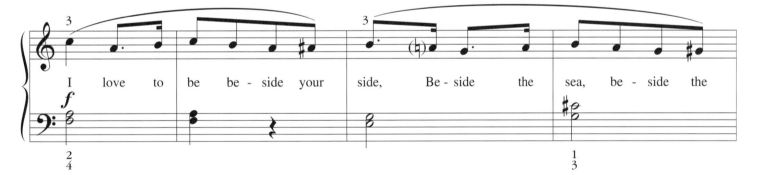

I love to be be - side your side, Be - side the sea, be - side the

sea - side,_____ By the beau - ti - ful sea._____

Ain't We Got Fun

words and music by
Gus Kahn, Raymond B. Egan
and **Richard Whiting**
arr. by **Geoffrey Haydon**
and **James Lyke**

Moderato

mf Ev - 'ry morn - ing, Ev - 'ry eve - ning, Ain't we got fun,

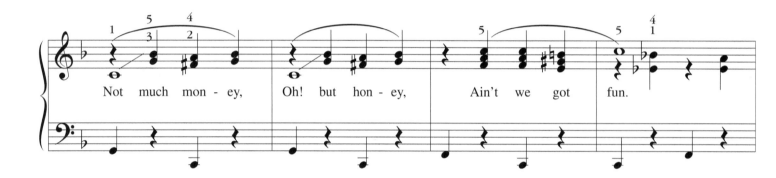

Not much mon - ey, Oh! but hon - ey, Ain't we got fun.

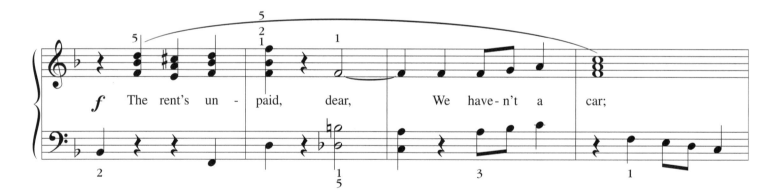

f The rent's un - paid, dear, We have - n't a car;

mf But an - y - way dear, We'll stay as we are.

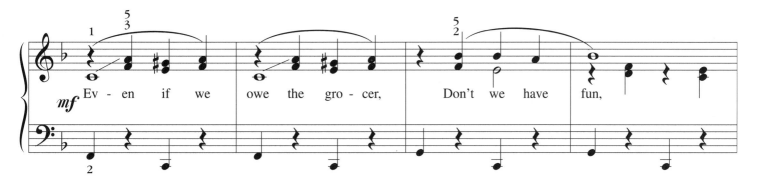

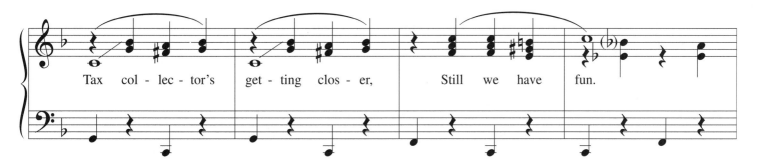

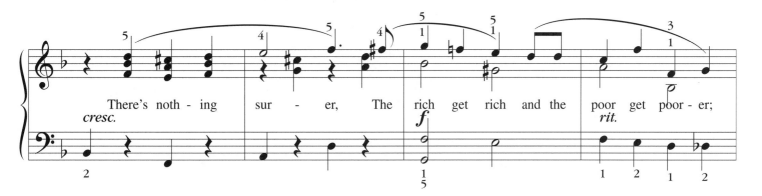

Carolina In The Morning

words by **Gus Kahn**
music by **Walter Donaldson**
arr. by **Geoffrey Haydon**
and **James Lyke**

Moderato

Noth- ing could be fin- er than to be in Car- o- lin- a in the morn - ing.

No- one could be sweet- er than my sweet- ie when I meet her in the morn - ing.

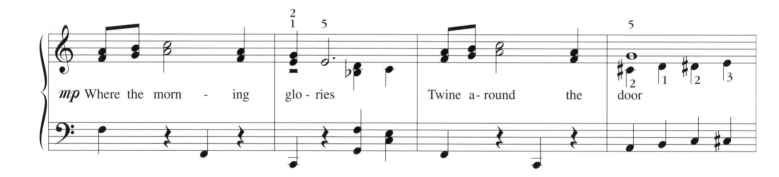

mp Where the morn - ing glo - ries Twine a- round the door

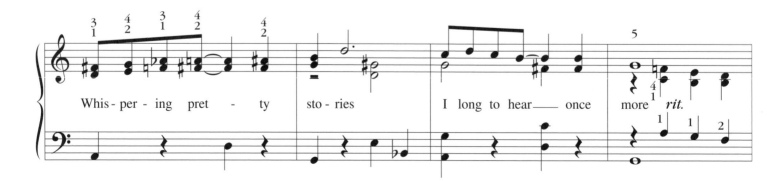

Whis- per- ing pret - ty sto - ries I long to hear___ once more *rit.*

a tempo

Stroll-ing with my girl-ie where the dew is pearl-y ear-ly in the morn - ing

But-ter-flies all flut-ter up and kiss each lit-tle but-ter-cup at dawn - ing

If I had A-lad-din's lamp for on-ly a day___ I'd make a wish and here's what I'd say___

Noth-ing could be fin-er than to be in Car-o-lin-a in the morn — — ing.

Say It With Music

words and music by **Irving Berlin**
arr. by **Geoffrey Haydon**
and **James Lyke**

Moderato (♩ = 120–130)

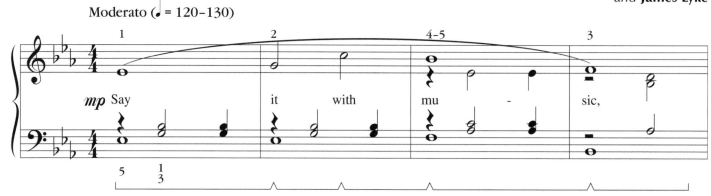

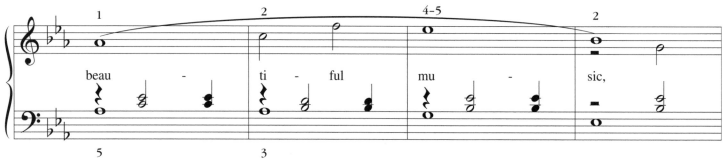

ped. simile

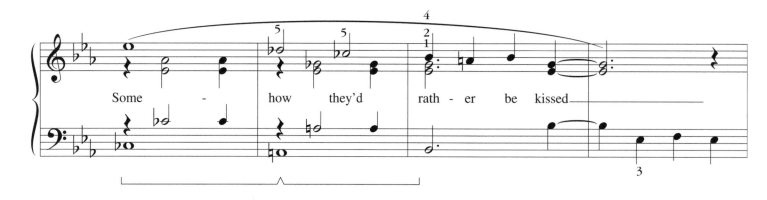

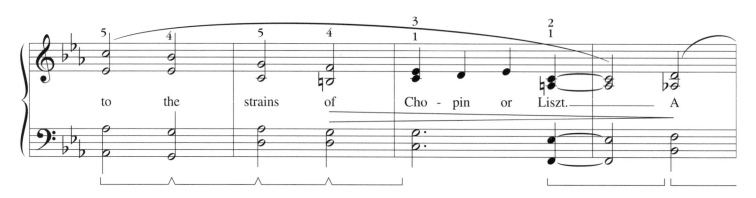

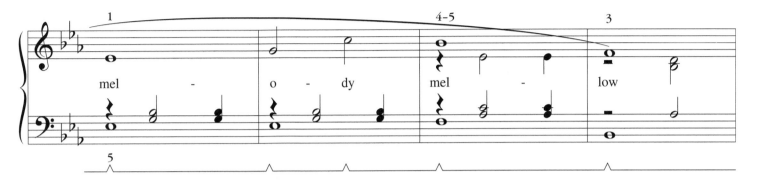

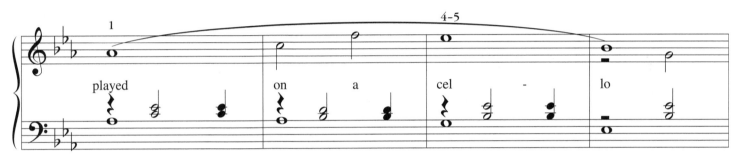

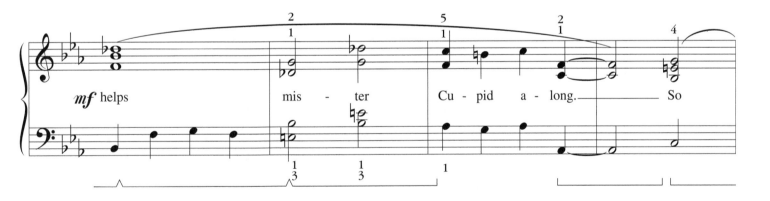

Oh! How I Hate To Get Up In The Morning

words and music by **Irving Berlin**
arr. by **Geoffrey Haydon**
and **James Lyke**

got to get up, You've got to get up, You've got to get up this morn - ing!"

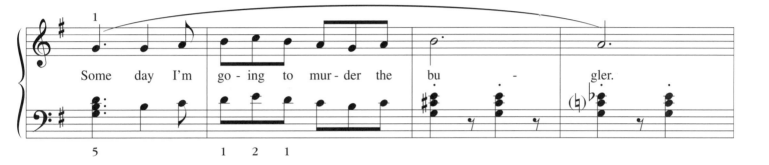

Some day I'm go - ing to mur - der the bu - gler.

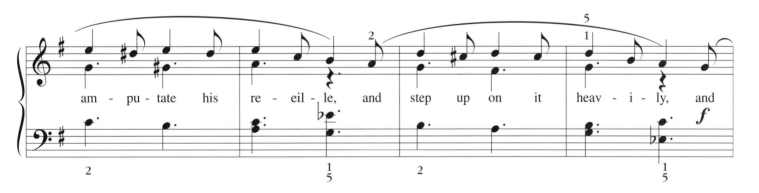

Some day they're go - ing to find him dead. *mf* I'll

am - pu - tate his re - eil - le, and step up on it heav - i - ly, and *f*

spend the rest of my life in bed.

Swanee

music by **George Gershwin**
words by **Irving Caesar**
arr. by **Geoffrey Haydon**
and **James Lyke**

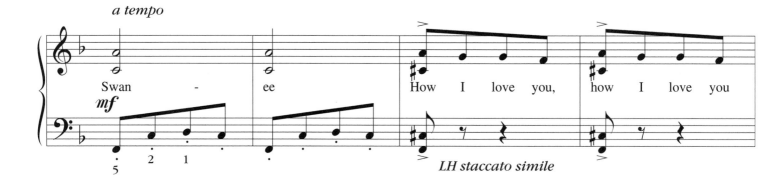

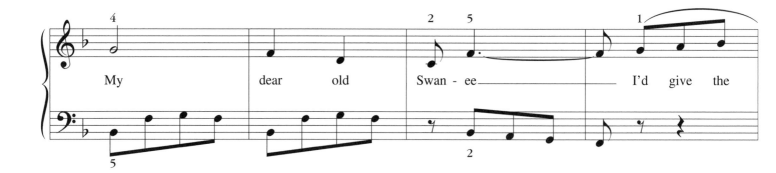

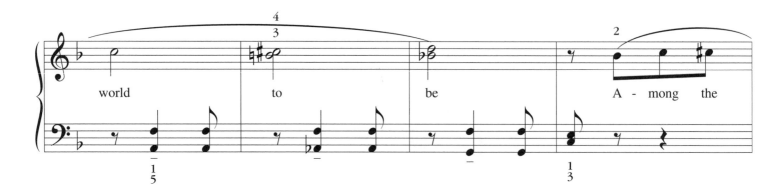

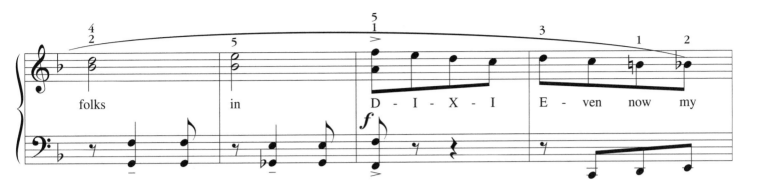

folks in D - I - X - I E - ven now my

Mam - my's wait - ing for me Pray - ing for me

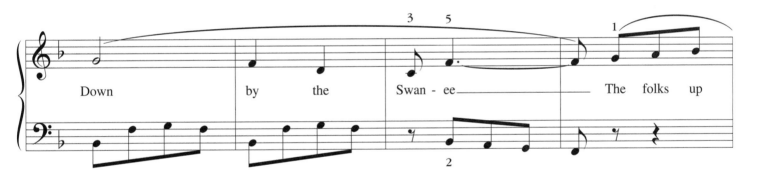

Down by the Swan - ee The folks up

north will see me no more When

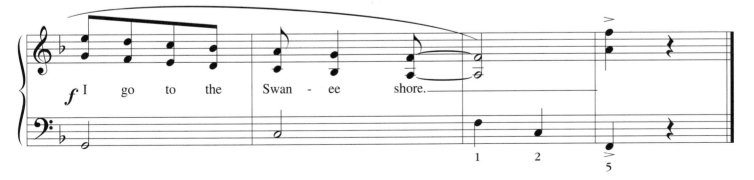

I go to the Swan - ee shore.

When I Lost You

words and music by **Irving Berlin**
arr. by **Geoffrey Haydon**
and **James Lyke**

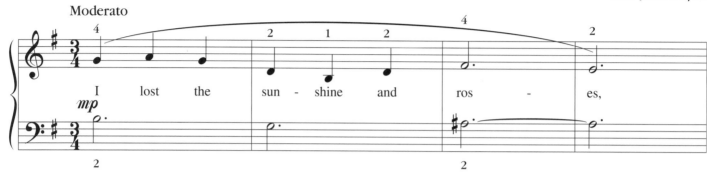

I lost the sun - shine and ros - es,

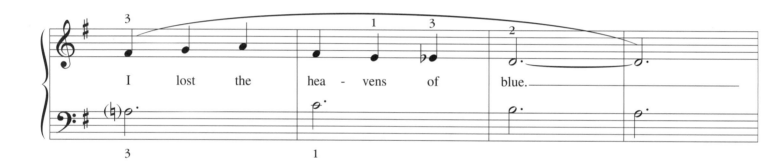

I lost the hea - vens of blue.

I lost the beau - ti - ful rain - bow,

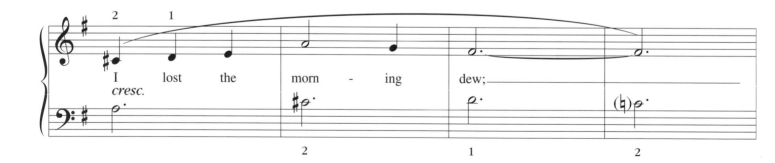

I lost the morn - ing dew;

2389

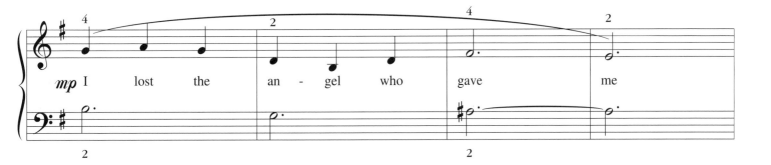

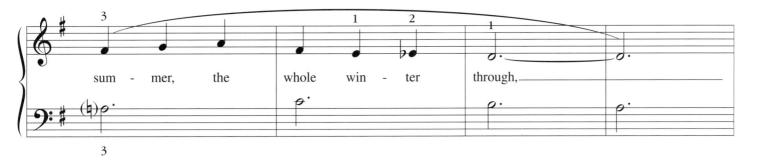

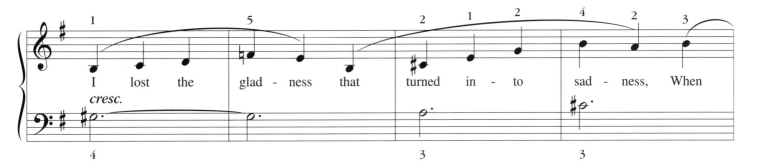

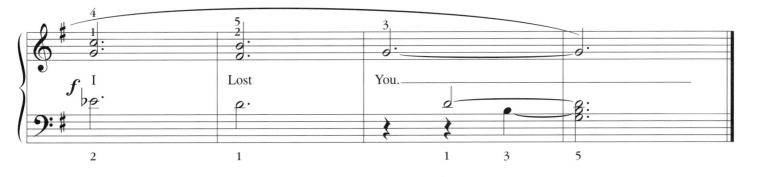

Till The Clouds Roll By
(Oh, Boy)

words by **P. G. Wodehouse**
music by **Jerome Kern**
arr. by **Geoffrey Haydon**
and **James Lyke**

vain_____ to re - main and chat - ter, And to

wait_____ for a clear - er sky;_____ Hel - ter

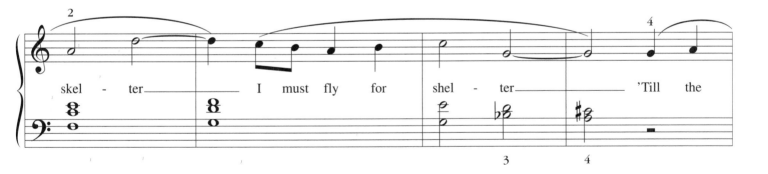

skel - ter_____ I must fly for shel - ter_____ 'Till the

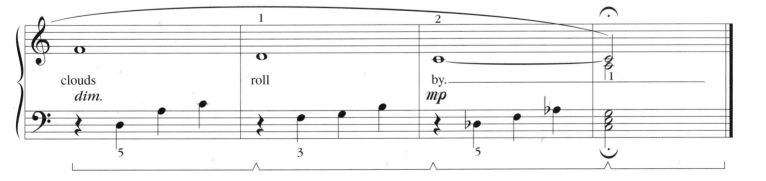

clouds roll by._____

dim. *mp*

OLDIES BUT GOODIES

CD ACCOMPANIMENT TRACKS

Each track contains a two bar count off. Upbeat values are included in the two measures.

CD tracks by Geoffrey Haydon